How to Sell Ice to Eskimos

175 Selling Skills You Should Know

Graham Watkins

ISBN-13:978-1545433775
ISBN-10:1545433771

Table of Contents

This little book is dedicated to the Salesmen and their Managers who came before me, who taught me, to those I worked with and learned from and to those Salesmen and Women who will come in the future.

As Henry Ford, of Ford Motor Company, famously said;

"Nothing happens until someone sells something."

Introduction

'You can't sell ice to Eskimos. Eskimos already have plenty of the stuff and selling someone a product they don't need is morally wrong,' I was once told by a rather pompous sales manager. In a way he was right, of course, no one should be selling useless unwanted products to anyone but at the same time he was mistaken. You can sell ice to Eskimos. Eskimos eat ice cream. When I pointed this obvious fact out to him he scoffed and changed the subject. It's an interesting argument and the reason I called this book 'How to Sell Ice to Eskimos.' Oh, and to grab your attention. Despite the title there are no Eskimos in the book just lots of strategies and ideas that will help you win more orders.

Some years ago I found myself at a crossroads in my life. After four years at sea as a marine engineer I wanted to come ashore. Then, I saw an advertisement in a national newspaper, 'Wanted ambitious young men to train as weighing machine salesmen'. The advert had been placed by W. & T. Avery Limited, the biggest scale manufacturer in Britain and, arguably, in the world. When I responded to that advertisement I had no comprehension of how it would change my life. The training that Avery gave me was archaic in style but it was effective. To join W. & T. Avery Limited or Averys as everyone called the company, was to join a group of people convinced that they were an elite and invincible force.

My career with Averys included industrial selling, sales management and the training of salesman. Later I worked for a Japanese company learning new techniques to deal with awkward sales and negotiations. I started my own company in 1989 which, thanks to the ideas you are about to read, grew into a multi million pound business which I then sold to a PLC. How did I do it? By using the tips and techniques of selling I have learned over the years. I've refined them into short bullet points that are easy to understand and remember.

This book isn't about getting customers and bashing them over the head until they buy. There are already hundreds written like that and most are nonsense produced by self proclaimed experts. Instead it's about refining your techniques so that sales are made quickly, calmly, and without any fuss. The resulting sales are pleasant for the customers, who don't feel they are being sold to and to you because the outcome is the one you want; an order. To keep things simple, I have dealt with the sequences of a sale in fourteen easy to understand stages plus an extra chapter where the tables are turned so we see things from the customers perspective and understand some of the ploys they might use to win an advantage.

One of the simplest closes, someone in sales can use, is the 'alternative close'. It's as old as the hills but it still works. Here goes. Imagine you're the customer, 'Which is more important to you, to close more deals or earn more money?' Both answers are, of course, in this book. With an alternative close, whatever the answer, everyone wins. If you want to be a winner, read on. Simple ideas like this are what make high flyers.

Graham Watkins
Garnlwyd 2014

Graham Watkins

1   Before you start selling.

Eleven important things you need to know and do before you start selling.

1. Only work for a company that you respect and are confident gives good value and service. Without that confidence your inner enthusiasm will never shine, your customer will see through you, you will lose business and quickly become demoralised.

2. If you find yourself selling a second rate or over priced product find another company to work for fast. I once worked for a solar panel company who were not nice people and whose products were overpriced. Believe me, I felt awful and soon packed the job in. Your reputation and integrity are worth more than selling shabby goods.

3. Learn everything you possibly can about the company you are going to represent. Knowledge is power and the more you learn, the more confident you will become.

4. Remember, your first sale is yourself. Learn to smile and act with confidence even when you are feeling nervous.

5. Study your products from every angle so that you know all their strengths and weaknesses.

6. Learn the benefits your customers will gain by using your products. Customers buy benefits not features.

7. Research your competitors and their products. You can only beat your opponents when you understand them and are able to exploit their weaknesses. I learned the importance of this lesson while working for Averys in Maidstone where I was tasked with taking on a very competent adversary.

8. Find out about your customers, what problems and wants they have, that your product will satisfy. Without this essential knowledge you will rarely make a sale. If you understand your customer's business good communication and mutual respect follows.

9. Prepare your sales story in advance and rehearse, rehearse, rehearse.

10. Plan you sales campaign for efficiency and to maintain the momentum and energy you will need to hit your targets.

11. Let your inner enthusiasm, excitement and confidence shine out, like a beacon for all to see.

Graham Watkins

2   Twelve tips for opening the sale.

Making the first approach is one of the hardest parts of selling, often passed on to professional canvassers. We have all had the annoying phone calls during an evening meal. A good salesman may use these appointments but I prefer to develop my own customer base using referrals and other tools to find new clients.

1. Start by finding the right person, the one with the money and the authority to buy. Don't waste your time selling to intermediaries and underlings.

2. Intermediaries and underlings can help or hinder you so always treat them with courtesy and respect.

3. Open the sale with a question lid lifter. "Mr. Customer, are you interested in saving money?" "Have you thought about how to make your job easier?" "Is family security important to you?" "Would you like to reduce you service costs and downtime?" Question lid lifters need to be closed questions - ones that can only be answered yes or no - designed to give the answer that leads on to the next stage of the sale.

4. Make your initial approach interesting, relevant and designed to gain agreement.

5. Make the customer curious enough to want to know more. Tell him you can show him the solution to a problem he has, a new product that his competitors are using or a means of cutting costs.

6. VIP your way in with the appearance of importance. You only get one chance to make a good first impression. Quality clothes and a positive posture will give you credibility. Appear to be a prosperous salesman not a third rate hanger on?

7. Power your way in with the strength of an appointment.

8. When on the phone, use an alternative close to make you appointment. "Is Tuesday morning OK Mr. Customer or would Wednesday afternoon be better." Good alternative closes are answered yes or yes.

9. Never sell under adverse conditions. The customer may be taking delivery of a large order or dealing with some kind of emergency. If you don't have his full concentration or are standing in a busy corridor you will not get an order. If the conditions are wrong stop selling and make another appointment.

10. Use third party introductions to open the door for you. Existing customer referrals break down natural barriers. "Mr. Smith suggested that I contact you because…."

11. If you are rebuffed, don't lose heart. Lick your wounded pride and move on to your next prospect.

12. When you have finished for the day always make at least one extra call before you head home.

3   Twelve techniques and tips to help you present your product.

1. A demonstration is the best way to show what you have to offer.

2. Make your demonstration logical.

3. Explain every feature and convert them all to benefits. "The benefit of that feature Mr. Customer is that it saves you valuable time".

4. Button the sale with benefits. Remember customers buy benefits they don't buy features.

5. Use visual anchors to fix the benefits in the customers mind. Tell the customer the benefit, show him and tell him what you have just shown him. Good teachers have done this for years.

6. Check your customer understands and values each benefit. "Do you agree that would benefit you Mr. Customer?"

7. Focus on the unique features and benefits of your product; these are the ones that will blow out your competition.

8. Involve the customer and maintain his interest. Get him to touch and feel your product.

9. If your customer asks a diversionary question either answer it briefly and continue your presentation where you stopped or, if the question is irrelevant, say you will come to that point later. If the question was unimportant, the customer will soon forget it.

10. Keep watching your customer and listening for feedback.

11. If there is an interruption ask the customer, "Where were we?" when you resume, to re-focus his attention.

12. Use visual aids to support your presentation. A picture is worth a thousand words.

13. Be prepared to stop your presentation if the customer gives you a buying signal. Carrying on presenting is overselling and could well cost you the sale.

4   Building Customer Confidence.

Building customer confidence is an area that even experienced salespeople sometimes neglect. When they fail to make a sale, despite explaining all the benefits, they often don't understand why. If the customer has any doubts or is not confident in you, your company or your product he will not buy.

1. Take the trouble to explain how your service support works.

2. Tell your customer about the strengths of your company.

3. Demonstrate the quality of your product.

4. Tell the customer about yourself and why you like working for your company.

5. Never mention the name of any competitor.

6. Never criticise a competitor or their products. It sounds cheap and unprofessional.

7. Never knock your own company, your services or your products. To do so is disloyal and the kiss of death.

8. Always speak in a positive manner. The only thing more infectious than enthusiasm is a lack of enthusiasm.

9. Never argue with a customer. You will always lose even if you win the argument.

10. Always tell the truth and if you don't know something, admit it and find out the answer for your customer. He will respect your honesty.

5   Keeping control.

A sales call needs to go in the direction you plan if you want to reach your goal and do the deal. If you let your customer take control you are no longer selling, you are merely answering questions.

1. Seize the initiative right from the start with positive comments that you have prepared beforehand.

2. Avoid opening with idle chatter or jokes to break the ice. You are not a travelling storyteller and wasting time can easily annoy a busy customer.

3. Have the structure of the interview planned and rehearsed well beforehand.

4. Keep to the point and move forward in a logical and businesslike manner.

5. If the customer diverts you, keep calm and politely bring the meeting back on track.

6. Make sure the customer understands and agrees with each point. Use questions to check. 'Do you agree it will reduce the wastage Mr. Customer?' 'How much would that save you Mr. Customer?'

7. Use specific examples not generalisation. Don't say, 'Lots of factories use this machine.' It means nothing, instead name them and make sure they are similar to the prospect you are selling to.

8. Don't exaggerate, it demeans what you are saying and makes you less credible.

9. Avoid technical jargon that the customer may not understand. If he can't grasp the meaning of what you are saying or feels foolish because he doesn't know what you are talking about he won't buy.

10. Avoid flattery, wheedling, begging for the order or strong arm selling tactics. These are the tools of a shyster and not fit for the modern world.

11. Use a light touch. Make the customer believe he is buying from you, not being sold to.

6   Overcoming objections.

Selling is sometimes like being in an obstacle
race with customers constantly placing obstacles
and objections in your way. If you want to win
you must be able to get past the obstacles.
Many sales people are afraid of objections and
see them as a real problem. They aren't if you
use the right approach to deal with them.
Instead, think of objections as pointers to the
order you are about to win. Handled correctly,
objections can even be used to close the sale.

1. List all the objections you can think of and
   write down how you will handle each one.
   Every time you hear a new one, add it to
   the list. Test and refine your answers until
   before long you know how to deal with
   any objection you come across. You'll be
   surprised at how few there really are.

2. Keep calm and positive when handling
   objections. If you panic the sale is lost.

3. Restate the objection to make it easier to
   deal with. 'It's far too complicated for my
   staff,' could be restated as, 'so you
   believe that the right staff training is an
   important issue.' Rephrasing this way,
   allows the salesman to move on and
   explain how staff training can be included
   in the deal and thereby overcome the
   objection.

4. Don't argue or contradict the customer even when he raises a silly objection or is wrong. Even if you win the argument it is unlikely that you will get an order. A good way of overcoming this type of objection is to agree and then disagree using the words yes and but. If the customer tells a solar panel salesman, 'I don't want solar panels fixed to my slate roof in case it leaks,' might be answered, 'Yes Mr. Customer I understand your concern about the roof brackets but the way we fixing our brackets ensures the roof will never leak.' The salesman has agreed with the customer and now goes on to deal with the objection. Yes and but are valuable words when dealing with objections.

5. Agree with the objection and offer a compensating benefit. This approach is used where the objection is a minor one and unlikely to break the deal. The customer might say, 'I don't like the size of your display, its too big,' hard to argue with, so the salesman concedes and says, 'You are right Mr. Customer the display is large but there is a benefit to having a big display, it's easier to read and there will be less mistakes.'

6. Forestall the objection before it's raised by the customer. By building the answer to an objection into your presentation you keep control and help the presentation flow more smoothly. Waiting for the customer to raise objections runs the risk of allowing yourself to get side tracked. This approach should only be used with objections which you believe the customer will raise. Other objections that might not get mentioned should be left alone. Why make the job more difficult.

7. Use customer testimonials to answer objections. Testimonials are effective tools and a way for the salesman to stand back and let another client do the work. If, for example, a customer expresses concern about reliability the objection could be handled by producing a letter from an existing customer praising the equipment and quality of service he has experienced from your company.

8. Defer and move on. Sometimes customers like to throw spurious objections into the conversation many of which do not deserve answering. Indeed, to try and answer then may lead up a dead end and spoil the meeting. When this happens one strategy is to defer and

move on. If the customer says, 'X company's machine is smaller than yours,' referring to your competitor, it would be a mistake to engage in a debate about the size merits of either product. Instead answer, 'oh, really,' and carry on with your demonstration. If size is a serious issue the customer will raise it again. If not it will soon be forgotten.

9. One of my favourites is the boomerang. Use a boomerang to turn the apparent, and at first sight serious objection, into a possible order. 'Your price is too high,' might be boomeranged back as, 'are you saying that if we spread the cost you will go ahead and buy?'

7   Dealing with price.

1. Take the 'ice' out of price. If you have a complex about the price your customer will soon become price conscious. Never be afraid of price. Speak about it with fear free frankness.

2. Justify the price with benefits before you reveal it. If the customer asks the price at the beginning of your presentation suggest that you will come to it later and confidently carry on with explaining the benefits. You need to build desirability first so that the customer wants the product and price then has less significance. If the customer insists on knowing the price at the beginning, tell him confidently and carry on.

3. Spread the price thin, by breaking it down to a cost per day or per unit and relate the cost to the benefits over the same period.

4. If you are dealing with a price difference break that down in the same way to make it look smaller.

5. Draw parallels by comparing the daily or per unit price with an everyday expense. 'It's only the same as buying a litre of petrol a day.'

6. Use other high priced objects as a comparison.

7. If the customer asks the price and, having built some desire, you are ready to reveal it, ask, 'How do you want to pay?' This question can lead into a close, particularly if the enquiry is a buying sign - we will talk more about buying signs and closes later.

8. Is price the real issue or a smokescreen hiding the real objection? Maybe the customer does not feel confident in you, your company or your products benefits. The best way to find out is to ask him. 'Are you saying you can't see enough benefits in the product Mr. Customer?' 'Is it something about my company you are not sure about?' 'Is it me?' Teasing out the real objection gives you the opportunity to overcome it and move on.

9. Be prepared to stand your ground. The customer may have already decided to buy and is just pushing to see if he can get more discount.

10. If you are negotiating and offer a discount always ask for something in return. Never give a concession without getting something back. If the customer wants a

lower price, and it's in your power to give it, you might ask for payment with order, an introduction to two new prospective buyers or a bigger order. Failure to win a concession weakens your position and invites further demands.

Graham Watkins

8   Asking the right open questions.

For a sales interview to end in success the salesman needs to understand what interests the customer, what his problems are and what is likely to make him buy. Apart from research beforehand, the simplest way to find out is to ask questions. During a sales call, two types of questions are used depending on the purpose of the question. The first, an open question, is designed to elicit answers that give information. The second, a closed question, is used where the salesman is not looking for information but, instead, wants to nudge the customer in a particular direction. Closed questions are commonly used when making an initial approach or asking for the order. We will deal with closed questions later.

1. Open questions ask for information and are difficult to answer yes or no.

2. 'What do you think of the savings you will make when the new machine is working?'

3. 'Why do you do it that way?'

4. 'When will the factory be expanding?'

5. 'How soon will you want installation?'

6. 'Where do you think is the best place to do the training?'

7. 'Who is the best person to speak to about this?'

8. Rudyard Kipling explains open questions eloquently in his story 'The Elephant's Child.'

> I keep six honest serving men,
> (They taught me all I knew),
> Their names are What and Why and When
> And How and Where and Who.

9   Listening skills.

It's no good just asking the right questions. An essential skill every salesman needs to have is the ability to listen to the answers. Without it the salesman will not be able to interpret or respond properly to customers reactions. When this happens the presentation becomes a one sided communication, the salesman is telling the customer who quickly loses interest and tunes out. Telling isn't selling.

1. To be a good listener requires skill, practice and discipline. You can only listen properly when you can control your ego, your intellect, your emotions and your behaviour.

2. Successful listening needs complete attention, an interest in the person speaking and an open mind.

3. Because we think four times faster than people speak it is easy to get bored and switch off. Your customer may be dull or have nothing to say worth hearing but what he says can reveal the key to making the sale so you must listen carefully.

4. If he is giving you too many facts try and concentrate on the key issues. Ignore other points that are irrelevant to the sale.

5. If you don't understand or the customer is going too fast slow him down by asking questions.

6. Use the why question to expand the customers points.

7. Take a few notes of what he says.

8. If the issues are contentious avoid reacting immediately. Don't interrupt. Hear him out.

9. Listen with empathy. What mood is he in; is he angry, critical, optimistic or excited?

10. Use your body to listen, lean forward and maintain eye contact. Don't create a barrier by folding your arms.

11. Encourage your customer by staying neutral and offering interjections like, 'I see', 'that's interesting' and 'really.'

12. Summarise the main points raised by your customer to confirm you both agree. This is a good opportunity to rephrase them ready to be answered.

10   Body language.

As well as listening, the alert salesman has another means of reading the customer. Non verbal or body language can be particularly valuable in revealing insincerity when it contradicts what is being said.

1. If a salesman believes in what he is doing his body language will take care of itself.

2. Reinforce your body language by adopting an alert posture, lean forwards and maintain eye contact.

3. Avoid frowning or creating barriers by folding your arms.

4. Don't doodle, fidget, wave your arms about excitedly or bang the table to make your point.

5. Be careful not to make your customer feel uncomfortable by standing too close or touching more than is appropriate, a firm handshake is normally enough.

6. Watch for body language signals from the customer.

7. Is the customer fidgeting? He may be bored, uncomfortable or simply not listening to what you are saying.

8. Does he put his hand over his mouth when he speaks? If he does he might not be telling the truth.

9. Being unable to look you in the eye is another sign of dishonesty but it also suggests someone who lacks confidence or is feeling intimidated. You may need to back off and give him some space to make him feel more comfortable.

10. Is your customer looking happy or irritated, comfortable or bored? These are all signs that can be read and interpreted to a salesman's advantage.

11   Transactional Analysis.

The psychologist, Eric Berne developed the theory of transactional analysis. In it he explains that the human mind operates in multiple states or egos which can quickly change according to different stimuli. Put simply there are three main states; 'Adult' where the person is rational and capable of problem solving; 'Child' where the person becomes dependent, non-threatening, uninhibited and innocent, and; 'Parent' where the person is nurturing, critical and protective. These uses of the names adult, child and parent are different to our normal understanding of them. During a sales call, the customer might switch between any or all of these egos several times. If he wants to win an order, the salesman needs to recognise which ego he is dealing with and modify his approach accordingly. In addition, to make things a little more complicated, he needs to understand which ego is uppermost in his own mind. Not an easy trick.

1. To identify which ego is prevalent and understand the customer's behaviour the salesman needs to listen to the words used, the tone of voice and the customer's body language.

2. Confusing signals indicate that the customer's behaviour is fluctuating.

3. What the salesman says can change the customer's ego very quickly.

4. If the customer has adopted a 'Child' like ego he will be trusting, defiant, uninhibited, non-threatening, dependant and fun loving.

5. Signs of a 'Child' ego include dishonesty, sulking, whining, an inability to problem solve and spontaneity.

6. The customer showing a 'Parent' ego is protective, critical and sometimes bossy.

7. A 'Parent' ego is represented by impatience, taking charge and adverse comments.

8. A customer displaying an 'Adult' ego will be analytical, logical and a problem solver.

9. Signs of an 'Adult' ego include courtesy, the ability to listen and rational questioning.

10. In most circumstances, the salesman should maintain an 'Adult' ego, regardless of the mood of the customer.

11. Transactional analysis is an effective tool for understanding why the customer is behaving the way he is.

12. If you want to learn more, read Eric Berne's book 'The Games People Play'.

Graham Watkins

12   Buying signals.

One of the things the salesman needs to be listening and watching for is buying signals. These are comments or non verbal clues that indicate the customer is ready to place an order.

1. Buying signals are signposts to the sale.

2. They can come at any time.

3. Miss buying signals and you risk losing the order.

4. Some buying signals come in the form of a question. The customer might ask, 'How long is the delivery?' 'Are they available in red?' 'How long is the guarantee?' 'How much is it?'

5. Other buying signals may be apparent throw away comments that the customer makes, 'I like that.' 'The savings look great.' 'My staff would love to use it.'

6. Non verbal buying signs include things like the customer using the product during a demonstration or showing it to a staff member.

7. Learn to recognise buying signs.

8. When you hear or see a new buying signal make a mental note of it and write it

down after the sales call. Then devise a closing question to go with it.

9. Every time you hear a buying signal you must ask a closing question. If you don't, you are not doing your job properly.

13   Closing the sale.

Some salesmen are afraid of asking for an order. They either, don't want to upset the customer or lack the confidence to ask the important question - will you buy? As a result they go through life wondering why their performance is second rate, why their peers always sell more. What they need is an armoury of closing tools. Here are a few that I like to use.

1. Every time you hear a buying signal, ask a closing question. I've repeated it because it is so important. Do this and you will sell more.

2. Learn a variety of different closing questions so that you can ask repeatedly without sounding pushy.

3. Closing questions are framed to elicit a yes answer and are different to the open questions used to gather information.

4. Always be closing. If the customer gives you a buying signal as you walk in the door ask a closing question. If he buys you will save time and avoid overselling your product.

5. Ask for the order with questions like, 'Are you ready to go ahead Mr. Customer?' 'Can I take your order?' 'Shall I start doing the paperwork?'

6. When you ask closing questions, reinforce them by leaning forward smiling and nodding you head. If you have done your work properly the customer will mirror your actions and you will have an order.

7. Use an alternative close where you ask the customer if he wants to buy or he wants to buy. 'Would you like delivery on Tuesday or would Wednesday be better?' 'Are you paying cash or would you prefer to lease the machine?' 'Do you want the 3KW system or the 4KW one?' This close is also known as a 'Morton's Fork'. Morton, Henry VII's tax collector, used the same strategy and always levies the maximum tax possible.

8. Using a boomerang close involves taking a customer's objection you know you can overcome and turning it into a closing opportunity. The customer might object by saying, 'A one year guarantee doesn't give me much confidence.' Knowing that he has the option to offer an extended three year warranty the salesman is able to say, 'If I could extend the product guarantee an extra two years would you go ahead?'

9. Assume the customer is going to buy and start filling out the order form. If he isn't ready he will soon tell you. If he does stop you ask why and do some more selling. An assumptive close is a good way to expose an objection you might still need to deal with.

10. If you have a customer who is dithering, the 'Duke of Wellington Close' is a useful tool. Produce a sheet of paper and invite the customer to write down all the benefits of your offer on the left hand side. Make sure there are lots and don't forget to help him if he can't remember them all. Then, suggest he writes down all the reasons for not buying on the right hand side. He needs no help for this. Because the customer has been thinking about all the positives, he will find it difficult to switch to the negatives and very few will get written. Leave him a few moments and then go for an assumptive close. Either he will buy or you will have identified the final objection you need to overcome.

11. Another closing technique is the 'Snowball Close'. This involves asking a series of questions to create a snowballing sequence of yes answers something like this; 'You say you are

happy with training we offer Mr. Customer?' 'Yes.' 'You prefer the 3KW machine?' 'Yes.' 'Have we discussed everything we need to cover?' 'Yes.' 'Would delivery on Thursday be OK?' 'Yes.' The last question asked after several yes answers is, of course, the closing question. It is also possible to apply the same approach using a series of no answers and finishing along the lines of, 'So there is no reason you can't go ahead?'

12. Closing the major question using a minor issue is a style of closing where a minor question is asked which by its nature says the customer is going ahead. For example you might ask, 'Is delivery next Thursday early enough for you?' If the customer says yes he is also saying yes I want it without you asking him to buy.

13. Once the customer has agreed to buy, complete the paperwork quickly, thank him for the business, exchange a few general pleasantries and leave. Do not continue to sell after the customer has said yes. If you do, you run the risk of raising an issue that may cause the customer to change his mind.

14. Don't make your closing questions complicated. Keep them simple and tailor them to the buying signal you have just been given. Here are a few examples that I like to use;

Customer's buying signal	Salesman's closing question
'How long is the delivery?'	'When do you want it?'
'Do you do them in red?'	'Do you want a red one?'
'How long is the guarantee?'	'Twelve months from delivery. When would you like it to be delivered?'
'What's the price?'	'How are you going to pay?'
'The display is too small.'	'If I can supply a model with a larger display will you buy it?' (Boomerang)
'I like the speed. It will save a lot of time.'	'What's your full address Mr. Customer?' (Producing an order form.)

Graham Watkins

14   Negotiating.

Once the buyer has satisfied himself that, in principle, he wants to go ahead the sale may move on to a different phase. This is where the final details of the deal are worked out through a series of negotiations. During a negotiation both the seller and the buyer are looking to balance the deal to make it equitable for their side.

1. Any negotiation should begin with a review of what has already been achieved. The customer has found a product or service he wants and the salesman has found a customer.

2. At this stage keep the mood positive and avoid any arguments. Go over the history and encourage the customer to respond.

3. The salesman's first objective is to get all the issues that need discussing out into the open. Until both sides agree they have defined all the points to be negotiated, avoid any detailed discussion.

4. Use the issue list to make an agenda. Begin with easier items that can quickly be resolved. These so called 'bridging items' will help create an atmosphere of partnership.

5. Keep the more contentious points back to be dealt with later.

6. Refine the issues into terms that both sides understand and agree on.

7. Start working through the agenda and be prepared to give and receive concessions.

8. Understand your fall back positions and what your limits are. If the customer is not prepared to meet them be prepared to walk away and break the deal.

9. Use 'Trial Balloons' to test proposals without making a commitment. 'What if we…'

10. Ask for mutually profitable trade offs in return for concessions.

11. Retreat to your fall back positions slowly, while showing the pain you are feeling.

12. Refer to a higher authority if you need time to think.

13. Summarise regularly to remind the customer how much he has won from you.

14. Ask your customer for help if the demand he is making is not possible.

15. As each item is dealt with confirm what has been agreed and make notes.

16. If the customer springs a surprise item, remind him that all the items should have been declared at the beginning and be prepared to revisit earlier points on the agenda.

17. Keep calm and if an item is proving difficult suggest that it is deferred until later on.

18. Never say no. Instead use a three stage refusal. See their point, give your position and propose an alternative way forward.

19. Be prepared to stand firm.

20. Aim to conclude the negotiation so that both sides achieve a profitable outcome.

15   Buyer's secret weapons.

Buyers use a variety of strategies to improve their negotiating position, dislocate the salesman's flow and win extra concessions. Here are just a few of them.

1. Take me to your leader. A good buyer will often try to optimise the rank of the salesman since a more senior person will have more authority to give discount and offer better terms.

2. Good guy bad guy, two buyers operating together to disorientate the salesman. This ploy, used by a well known supermarket chain, where a senior buyer interrupts a sales call, complains about the salesman's company and tells the junior buyer to see him afterwards.

3. Geronimo's scalps; where a buyer leaves a competitor's quotation in partial view on his desk, to put extra pressure on the salesman.

4. The whoopee cushion; positioning the salesman on an uncomfortable chair looking into the sun.

5. List of grievances; where the buyer starts the interview by complaining about the salesman's company.

6. Pavlov's dog; The Russian Physiologist, Ivan Pavlov experimented with dogs to condition their behaviour. This buyer's strategy is to keep changing the subject during a sales presentation with the intention of confusing and disorientating the salesman.

7. Good news bad news; where the buyer says, 'You've got the order but we just need to change a few things'.

8. The wince; often used to try and get a lower price.

9. I don't speak the language or Danish Gambit; where the buyer appears not to understand what the salesman is talking about. A Danish Gambit is also an opening chess strategy.

10. Let you and him fight; Sending the salesman away to do battle with his boss and get a better deal.

11. Save the cherry till last; the buyer elicits the best deal he can and then surprises the salesman with a question like, 'What if I increase the size of the order?'

12. Salami; a way of winning a series of small concessions like slices of salami until a

huge chunk of the sausage, or possibly price, has been eroded.

13. Would you like time to think? Where the salesman is left hanging to see if he will give a better price or improve his offer in some other way.

14. Guess who that was on the phone? Where the buyer waits until the end of the negotiation and then suggests that he has just had another possibly better offer.

That's about the sum of it. Selling isn't hard once you learn and employ the tips I have shared in this little book.

Graham Watkins

If you found the ideas in How to Sell Ice to Eskimos useful, a review would be greatly appreciated. Also, you might like to read another, rather larger, book of mine, Exit Strategy - A practical guide to selling your business, describing how I took the next step and sold my successful company to a PLC and rode into the sunset.

Here's what a few people have said about Exit-Strategy;

"If you are in business and want a happy ending, I recommend that you read this book."

Phil Oliver - Senior Partner - UHY Hacker Young.

"In Exit Strategy Graham Watkins delivers solutions to business problems you don't even know exist. The knowledge he shares in this book is worth thousands of pounds."

Dr. Robert Hughes Jones BSc. MSc. Phd. Cantab. - Research Director - Slumberger Cambridge Research Limited.

"Exit Strategy is a really good read and packed with valuable ideas.'

Philip Sibson - Sales Director - Aquilla Business Products.

Learn more....

Graham Watkins

Foreword

When my wife and I decided to sell our business in 2000 we had no idea what was involved. Scouring libraries for good advice on the subject and talking to professionals we quickly realised what a big project selling up is and that there is very little written on the subject that the entrepreneur, who is not a book worm, can turn to for help.

If, like me, you have a short attention span and prefer to make decisions while things are happening you will appreciate why many business owners make a mess of the last big part of their career, selling up. To do the job properly takes time, in our case three years from making the decision to finally walking away. During those three years we made a lot of mistakes and went through a meteoric learning curve. There were a number of false starts, dashed hopes and tears on more than one occasion.

We were fortunate in the choices of our financial and legal advisors. Their calm and reason helped keep things in perspective when everything seemed to be going wrong. I am indebted to my wife for helping me stay focussed throughout, to Phil Oliver of UHY Hacker Young Chartered Accountants and Robert Cawdron of Acton's Solicitors for having the patience to explain the complex issues we were dealing with and for offering good advice that enabled us to work our way slowly to a sale which, I believe, was satisfactory for all sides involved.

This book is not a record of the sale of our business; indeed the confidentiality agreement, our purchasers insisted on, does not allow it. Instead it is my views, based on personal experience, of what is involved in selling a company. I do not pretend 'Exit Strategy' is a textbook. Others far more qualified than me have already written mighty tomes on the subject and these are available to the scholars and academics for debate. The audience I have written for are those of us who are involved in owning and building businesses; people that get on and do things, the backbone of UK Plc.

I should acknowledge and thank my friend Dave Simkins FCCA and Phil Oliver, Senior Partner at UHY Hacker Young for their comments and suggestions regarding the content of this book together with the input of my cousin Graham Watkins and his wife Avis. Their gentle corrections of my appalling grammar helped teach me where to stick my commas.

Since I do not claim to be an expert, I recommend that you take professional advice before making any important decisions about selling a business.

If, as you read this book, you learn something that helps you sell your business successfully I will be pleased. I hope you enjoy the read. I certainly enjoyed writing it.

Graham Watkins
Garnlwyd

Exit Strategy is available as an eBook, paperback and an audio book.

Other books by Graham Watkins include;

The Sicilian Defence
The Iron Masters
A White Man's War
The Welsh Folly Book
Welsh Legends and Myths
Birth of a Salesman
The Enemy Within

Learn more at www.grahamwatkins.info

About the Author

After training as a marine engineer, Graham followed a successful career in sales and marketing until 1989 when he incorporated his own company, distributing retail and catering equipment.

The company grew and was sold in 2003 but the experience of dealing with the sale of the business made him realise how poorly prepared he was to make the most of the business which was his biggest asset. There was virtually nothing written to explain how to sell a company and the books that were available were mainly textbooks, written by accountants or lawyers.

Retired from business, he now lives with his wife in a rambling farmhouse in the Brecon Beacons and enjoys life, hobby-farming and writing.

Printed in Great Britain
by Amazon